HOW TO START A PROFITABLE SIDE HUSTLE

"Unlocking Financial Freedom through Smart Side-Hustle Strategies"

VINCENT SIM

Copyright ©

Dedication

"To those who dream of financial independence and dare to turn aspirations into actions. This book is dedicated to the ambitious souls embarking on the journey of starting a profitable side hustle—may your endeavors be fruitful, your resilience unwavering, and your path to success both rewarding and inspiring."

Table of Contents

Acknowledgments

"I express my deepest gratitude to all those whose support and encouragement made this book possible. Special thanks to my mentors for sharing invaluable insights, friends, and family for their unwavering belief, and the entrepreneurial community for fostering a spirit of innovation. Your collective influence has shaped these pages and, I hope, will guide countless others on the path to a successful and profitable side hustle."

Preface

Welcome to "How to Start a Profitable Side Hustle." In the evolving landscape of entrepreneurship, the concept of a side hustle has emerged as a powerful vehicle for financial growth and personal fulfillment. This book is a compass for those seeking to navigate the exciting terrain of creating a supplementary income stream.

As technology continues to redefine traditional employment models, the potential to carve out one's path becomes more accessible. Whether you are an aspiring entrepreneur, a full-time professional looking for extra income, or someone exploring passion projects, this guide is designed to equip you with practical strategies, insights, and a roadmap for launching and sustaining a profitable side hustle.

Throughout these pages, we'll delve into the nuances of identifying opportunities, understanding market dynamics, and developing the mindset crucial for entrepreneurial success. Drawing on real-world examples and proven methodologies, this book aims to demystify the process and empower you to tap into the world of profitable side hustles.

Remember, this is not just a manual; it's a companion on your journey toward financial independence and creative fulfillment. So, fasten your seatbelt and get ready to embark on a transformative adventure, where your side hustle isn't just about making money—it's about creating a life of purpose and prosperity.

Best wishes on your entrepreneurial voyage!

[Vincent Sims]

Chapter 1.

Introduction

- Defining a Side Hustle

In the dynamic landscape of modern work, the term "side hustle" has gained prominence as a flexible and innovative approach to income generation. A side hustle refers to any legitimate venture or project pursued alongside a person's primary source of income, often a full-time job. Unlike traditional part-time work, a side hustle is driven by personal passion, skills, or entrepreneurial aspirations.

At its core, a side hustle is a means of diversifying income streams, creating financial resilience, and pursuing individual interests outside the constraints of a traditional 9-to-5 job. It's a dynamic concept that adapts to the unique goals and circumstances of individuals, offering the freedom to explore creative endeavors or monetize skills in a way that aligns with personal values.

Side hustles come in various forms, from freelance work and consulting to selling handmade crafts or launching an online business. They provide an avenue for individuals to experiment with entrepreneurial ideas, test the market, and gradually transition from a conventional employment model to a more self-directed and fulfilling career path.

Importantly, a side hustle is not just about making extra money; it's a platform for personal and professional growth. It allows individuals to cultivate new skills, expand their network, and gain valuable experience in areas they are passionate about. The autonomy and ownership that come with a side hustle can be empowering, fostering a sense of control over one's financial destiny.

In a world where job security is increasingly uncertain, a well-nurtured side hustle can serve as a safety net, offering financial stability and the potential for long-term wealth creation. As we explore the strategies for starting a profitable side hustle, understanding the essence of what a side hustle is and the opportunities it presents lays the foundation for a journey toward financial independence and personal fulfillment.

- The Benefits of Starting a Side Hustle

Embarking on the journey of a side hustle offers a myriad of advantages that extend far beyond the realm of additional income. Whether fueled by passion, a desire for financial independence, or the pursuit of personal growth, the benefits are diverse and impactful.

1. Supplementary Income:
   - Perhaps the most obvious benefit, a side hustle provides an extra source of income, contributing to financial stability and offering a buffer against economic uncertainties.

2. Diversification of Income Streams:
   - Relying solely on a single income source can be risky. A side hustle acts as a supplementary revenue stream, diversifying

your financial portfolio and reducing dependency on a primary job.

3. Skill Development:

- Engaging in a side hustle allows you to acquire and refine a diverse set of skills. Whether it's marketing, customer service, or financial management, the hands-on experience can be invaluable for personal and professional growth.

4. Entrepreneurial Experience:

- For those aspiring to entrepreneurship, a side hustle serves as a low-risk testing ground. It provides insights into running a business, understanding market dynamics, and developing an entrepreneurial mindset.

5. Flexibility and Autonomy:

- Unlike traditional employment structures, side hustles often afford greater flexibility. You have the autonomy to choose when and where you work, fitting your entrepreneurial pursuits into your existing lifestyle.

6. Passion Pursuit:

- Many side hustles stem from personal interests and passions. This not only makes the work more enjoyable but can lead to a sense of purpose and fulfillment beyond the financial rewards.

7. Networking Opportunities:

- Building a side hustle often involves connecting with others in your industry or community. This network can open doors to collaborations, partnerships, and future opportunities.

8. Resume Enhancement:

- A successful side hustle is a valuable addition to your resume. It demonstrates initiative, creativity, and an ability to manage multiple responsibilities—a compelling narrative for potential employers or clients.

9. Increased Financial Confidence:

- Successfully managing a side hustle can boost your financial confidence. Knowing that you have the skills to generate income independently contributes to a sense of control over your financial future.

10. Long-Term Wealth Creation:

- Beyond immediate financial gains, a strategically developed side hustle has the potential for long-term wealth creation. It can evolve into a full-fledged business or investment opportunity over time.

In essence, starting a side hustle is a transformative journey with benefits that extend beyond the balance sheet. It's an investment in yourself, offering a pathway to financial freedom, skill acquisition, and a more fulfilling professional life.

- Common Misconceptions and Challenges

While the allure of a side hustle is undeniable, navigating the path to success is not without its share of misconceptions and challenges. Understanding and addressing these aspects is crucial for aspiring entrepreneurs seeking to embark on the rewarding but demanding journey of starting a profitable side hustle.

1. Overnight Success:
    - Misconception: One of the prevalent misconceptions is that side hustles can lead to overnight success. In reality, building a sustainable and profitable venture takes time, dedication, and consistent effort.

2. Easy Money:

- Misconception: Some believe that a side hustle guarantees quick and effortless money. In truth, successful ventures require careful planning, market research, and the ability to adapt to changing circumstances.

3. Lack of Time:

- Challenge: Balancing a side hustle with a full-time job, family commitments, and personal life can be challenging. Time management becomes crucial to avoid burnout and ensure sustainable progress.

4. Unrealistic Expectations:

- Misconception: Expecting immediate financial returns or unrealistically high profits can lead to disappointment. It's essential to set realistic goals and understand that building a successful side hustle is a gradual process.

5. Fear of Failure:

- Challenge: The fear of failure can be paralyzing. Overcoming this challenge involves acknowledging that setbacks are a natural part of the entrepreneurial journey and offering valuable learning experiences.

6. Lack of Focus:
- Challenge: Some individuals struggle with maintaining focus, especially when juggling multiple responsibilities. Clearly defining goals and priorities helps in staying on course amid distractions.

7. Insufficient Planning:
- Challenge: Inadequate planning can hinder the growth of a side hustle. Entrepreneurs need to invest time in creating a solid business plan, identifying target markets, and understanding their competition.

8. Limited Resources:
- Challenge: Starting a side hustle often requires resourcefulness. Limited finances,

time, or expertise can be challenging obstacles that need creative solutions and strategic prioritization.

9. Work-Life Balance:

- Challenge: Achieving a healthy work-life balance is an ongoing struggle. Entrepreneurs need to establish boundaries to prevent burnout and maintain overall well-being.

10. Market Saturation:

- Challenge: Depending on the chosen niche, facing a saturated market can be a challenge. Distinguishing your side hustle through unique value propositions and effective marketing becomes essential.

Acknowledging these misconceptions and challenges is the first step toward overcoming them. A realistic mindset, coupled with resilience and a willingness to learn, equips aspiring entrepreneurs to navigate the complexities of starting a profitable side hustle and emerge stronger on the other side.

Chapter 2

Finding Your Passion and Skills

- Self-reflection and Identifying Interests

Embarking on the journey of starting a profitable side hustle begins with a fundamental exploration of your passions and skills. This self-reflective process serves as the cornerstone for a fulfilling and successful entrepreneurial endeavor.

1. Introspection:
   - Begin by engaging in introspection. Ask yourself what activities bring you joy, what you find yourself naturally drawn to, and what tasks you lose track of time doing.

Identifying your passions involves recognizing the activities that resonate with your core values and bring a sense of purpose.

2. Assessing Hobbies and Interests:
   - Consider your hobbies and interests outside of work. These areas often house untapped potential for a side hustle. Whether it's a creative pursuit, a sport, or a specific skill, these hobbies can be transformed into profitable ventures with the right approach.

3. Recognizing Skills:
   - Take inventory of your skills, both personal and professional. What are you exceptionally good at? These skills can range from technical expertise to soft skills like communication or problem-solving. Your unique skill set can become the foundation for a distinctive and marketable side hustle.

4. Seeking Feedback:

- Sometimes, others see our strengths more objectively than we do. Seek feedback from friends, colleagues, or mentors. They might provide insights into skills or talents you may not have fully acknowledged.

5. Identifying Patterns:

- Look for patterns in your life experiences. What recurring themes or activities have been present throughout various stages of your life? Patterns can unveil consistent interests and guide you toward a side hustle that aligns with your long-term passions.

6. Assessing Market Demand:

- While passion is crucial, it's essential to assess the market demand for your chosen niche. Research to understand if there is a viable market for your skills and interests. This intersection of passion and demand is where a profitable side hustle can truly thrive.

7. Experimentation:

- Don't be afraid to experiment. Try out different activities, projects, or business ideas related to your passions. This hands-on approach not only refines your understanding of what you enjoy but also helps you discover the practical aspects of turning your interests into a viable business.

8. Continuous Learning:

- Embrace a mindset of continuous learning. As you identify your passions and skills, stay open to acquiring new knowledge and refining existing abilities. The willingness to adapt and grow is integral to the long-term success of your side hustle.

Finding your passion and skills is not a one-time event but an evolving process. It requires self-awareness, a willingness to explore, and a commitment to personal and professional development. Armed with a clear understanding of your passions and skills, you lay the foundation for a side hustle that not only aligns with your core values but also has the potential to flourish in the marketplace.

- Assessing Your Skills and Strengths

The success of any side hustle is intricately tied to the skills and strengths you bring to the table. Conducting a thorough assessment of your capabilities not only forms the basis for a sustainable venture but also positions you to leverage your unique strengths in the entrepreneurial landscape.

1. Inventory of Skills:
   - Start by creating a comprehensive inventory of your skills. These encompass both hard and soft skills—technical

expertise, communication abilities, problem-solving acumen, leadership qualities, and any other competencies you possess.

2. Professional Experience:

- Reflect on your professional experience. What roles have you excelled in? What achievements stand out? Your past accomplishments often highlight specific skills that can be translated into a successful side hustle.

3. Passion Alignment:

- Identify the skills that align with your passions. While assessing your skills, consider which ones bring you the most joy and fulfillment. A side hustle rooted in both skill and passion has a higher chance of sustainability.

4. Recognizing Transferable Skills:

- Recognize transferable skills that can be applied across different domains. These versatile skills, such as project management or problem-solving, can open up a range of side hustle possibilities beyond your current expertise.

5. Feedback from Others:
   - Seek feedback from colleagues, friends, or mentors. External perspectives can provide insights into your strengths that you might not be fully aware of. Their observations may reveal unique strengths that set you apart.

6. Skill Development Opportunities:
   - Identify areas for skill development. While assessing your current skills, also recognize the growth potential. Continuous learning and skill enhancement contribute to the adaptability and long-term viability of your side hustle.

7. Prioritization:
   - Prioritize your skills based on relevance to your side hustle goals. Not all skills may

be equally beneficial for your chosen venture. Focus on honing and leveraging the skills that directly contribute to the success of your entrepreneurial endeavor.

8. Niche Specialization:

- Assess if you have a specialization or niche expertise. Specialized skills often lead to unique value propositions, setting your side hustle apart in a competitive market.

9. Resourcefulness:

- Evaluate your resourcefulness and ability to navigate challenges. Entrepreneurship often demands resilience and creative problem-solving. Your capacity to adapt and overcome obstacles is a valuable strength.

10. Networking Abilities:

- Consider your networking abilities. Building connections within your industry or community is a skill that can facilitate partnerships, collaborations, and business growth.

Assessing your skills and strengths is not just about understanding what you can do; it's about strategically leveraging these assets to build a thriving side hustle. As you embark on this entrepreneurial journey, a clear awareness of your capabilities empowers you to make informed decisions, capitalize on opportunities, and navigate challenges with confidence.

- Matching Passion with Profitability

The intersection of passion and profitability is a pivotal point in the journey of starting a side hustle. While pursuing what you love is fulfilling, aligning that passion with viable business opportunities creates the foundation for a sustainable and successful venture.

1. Identifying Core Passions:

- Begin by identifying your core passions. What activities bring you joy and a deep sense of fulfillment? Whether it's a hobby, a cause, or a specific interest, understanding your genuine passions is the first step toward a purpose-driven side hustle.

2. Market Research:

- Conduct thorough market research to assess the demand for your passion. Evaluate if there is a target audience willing to pay for products or services related to your interests. A profitable side hustle requires a market that values what you love.

3. Analyzing Trends:

- Stay abreast of industry trends and changes. What may be a passionate pursuit today could evolve into a profitable venture tomorrow based on shifting consumer needs or emerging market trends.

4. Unique Value Proposition:

- Define your unique value proposition. How does your passion solve a problem or meet a need in the market? Clearly articulating the value you bring helps distinguish your side hustle in a competitive landscape.

5. Monetization Strategies:

- Explore various monetization strategies. From product sales and services to affiliate marketing or online courses, understanding how to turn your passion into a revenue stream is crucial for long-term sustainability.

6. Balancing Passion and Profit:

- Find the balance between what you love and what the market demands. This equilibrium ensures that your side hustle is not only financially viable but also resonates authentically with your interests.

7. Testing and Iterating:

- Test your ideas and be willing to iterate. Launching a minimum viable product or service allows you to gather feedback and refine your offerings based on customer responses. This iterative process is integral to the evolution of a profitable side hustle.

8. Scaling Opportunities:

- Assess scaling opportunities. As your side hustle gains traction, explore avenues for growth without compromising the essence of your passion. This may involve expanding offerings, entering new markets, or building strategic partnerships.

9. Aligning with Values:

- Ensure that your side hustle aligns with your values. A venture rooted in authenticity and genuine passion not only enhances your satisfaction but also resonates with customers who appreciate sincerity.

10. Sustainable Impact:

- Consider the long-term impact of your side hustle. A sustainable business model takes into account environmental, social, and economic considerations. Aligning your passion with a positive impact contributes to the overall success and fulfillment of your venture.

By meticulously matching passion with profitability, you create a side hustle that is not only financially rewarding but also personally fulfilling. It's a journey that harmonizes your authentic interests with the dynamic opportunities of the market, fostering a venture that stands the test of time.

Chapter 3.

Market Research and Opportunity Identification

- Understanding Market Trends

In the ever-evolving landscape of business, staying attuned to market trends is a crucial aspect of launching and sustaining a profitable side hustle. A keen understanding of market dynamics empowers entrepreneurs to identify opportunities, navigate challenges, and make informed decisions that contribute to the long-term success of their ventures.

1. Continuous Market Research:

- Engage in continuous market research to stay informed about evolving trends. Regularly monitor industry publications, news, and reports to identify shifts in consumer behavior, emerging technologies, and other relevant factors shaping your market.

2. Consumer Preferences:

- Pay close attention to changing consumer preferences. Understanding what customers value, desire, and prioritize provides insights into potential gaps in the market that your side hustle can fill.

3. Technology Impact:

- Recognize the impact of technology on your industry. Whether it's advancements in e-commerce, artificial intelligence, or digital marketing, staying technologically savvy positions your side hustle to capitalize on emerging opportunities.

4. Competitor Analysis:

- Conduct thorough competitor analysis to understand what similar businesses are doing. Identify their strengths, weaknesses, and strategies. This analysis not only informs your approach but can unveil untapped market niches.

5. Industry Reports and Studies:

- Leverage industry reports and studies. These resources provide in-depth insights into market trends, consumer behavior, and forecasts. Utilize such data to make informed decisions about your side hustle strategy.

6. Social and Cultural Shifts:

- Consider social and cultural shifts. Changes in societal values, lifestyles, or cultural preferences can significantly impact market trends. Adapting your side hustle to align with these shifts enhances its relevance and appeal.

7. Niche Identification:

- Identify niche markets within your industry. Understanding specialized segments allows you to tailor your products or services to meet specific needs, often with less competition and higher customer loyalty.

8. Online Presence Monitoring:

- Monitor your online presence. Social media platforms, customer reviews, and online forums provide real-time feedback on consumer sentiments and can serve as indicators of broader market trends.

9. Regulatory Changes:

- Stay informed about regulatory changes. Shifts in laws and regulations can influence market trends and present new challenges or opportunities. Being proactive in adapting to these changes is crucial for sustained success.

10. Flexibility and Adaptability:

- Cultivate a mindset of flexibility and adaptability. Markets are dynamic, and trends can change rapidly. A willingness to adjust your side hustle strategy based on evolving market dynamics ensures resilience and competitiveness.

Understanding market trends is not a one-time activity but an ongoing process integral to the entrepreneurial journey. By embracing a proactive approach to market analysis, entrepreneurs can position their side hustles to not only respond to current trends but also anticipate and capitalize on future opportunities in a rapidly changing business landscape.

- Identifying Niche Opportunities

In the vast landscape of entrepreneurship, finding and capitalizing on niche opportunities is often the key to a successful and sustainable side hustle. Niche markets represent specific segments with unique needs, allowing entrepreneurs to tailor their products or services for a specialized audience. Here's a guide to identifying and tapping into niche opportunities for your side hustle:

1. Market Research:
   - Begin with thorough market research. Identify industries or sectors where there might be an unmet need or an underserved audience. Look for gaps in existing offerings that your side hustle could fill.

2. Passion Alignment:

- Align niche opportunities with your passions and interests. Combining your genuine enthusiasm with a specialized market segment not only enhances your motivation but also fosters a deeper understanding of the niche.

3. Target Audience Identification:
   - Clearly define your target audience within the niche. Understand their demographics, preferences, and pain points. Tailoring your offerings to a specific audience ensures a more effective and personalized approach.

4. Competition Analysis:
   - Analyze the competition within the niche. Identify existing businesses catering to the same audience and evaluate their strengths and weaknesses. This analysis helps you position your side hustle uniquely.

5. Uniqueness Proposition:

- Develop a unique value proposition. Clearly articulate what sets your side hustle apart within the niche. This could be innovative features, superior quality, exceptional customer service, or any other factor that distinguishes your offerings.

6. Problem Solving:
   - Consider how your side hustle can solve a specific problem or address a pain point within the niche. A problem-solving approach not only enhances your value but also creates a more compelling reason for customers to choose your products or services.

7. Trends and Predictions:
   - Stay abreast of industry trends and predictions. Anticipating future needs within a niche allows you to position your side hustle as a forward-thinking solution, staying ahead of the curve.

8. Niche Validation:

- Validate the viability of the niche. Assess the demand for your offerings by conducting surveys, seeking feedback, or launching a pilot project. This validation process ensures that there is a genuine market for your niche.

9. Networking within the Niche:
- Build connections within the niche. Attend industry events, join relevant online communities, and engage with potential customers. Networking provides insights, builds credibility, and opens doors to collaboration opportunities.

10. Scalability Consideration:
- Evaluate the scalability of your side hustle within the niche. While starting small can be advantageous, ensuring that there is room for growth and expansion is essential for long-term success.

Identifying niche opportunities requires a combination of research, creativity, and a deep understanding of both the market and your passions. By carefully selecting a niche that aligns with your expertise and the unique needs of a specific audience, you position your side hustle for success in a competitive business landscape.

- Analyzing Competition and Gaps in the Market

A thorough analysis of competition and market gaps is a crucial step in shaping a successful side hustle. Understanding who you're up against and identifying unmet needs in the market allows you to position your venture strategically and offer something unique. Here's a guide to effectively analyze competition and discover gaps in the market:

1. Competitive Landscape Assessment:

- Begin by conducting a comprehensive assessment of the competitive landscape. Identify direct and indirect competitors, studying their products, services, pricing strategies, and overall market positioning.

2. Strengths and Weaknesses Analysis:

- Evaluate the strengths and weaknesses of your competitors. Understanding what they excel at and where they fall short provides insights into areas where your side hustle can differentiate itself.

3. Customer Reviews and Feedback:

- Dive into customer reviews and feedback for your competitors. Analyzing what customers appreciate or dislike about existing offerings can reveal opportunities to address unmet needs or improve upon existing solutions.

4. Market Trends and Innovations:

- Stay abreast of market trends and innovations. Analyze how your competitors are adapting to changing consumer preferences and technological advancements. Identify areas where your side hustle can leverage emerging trends.

5. Unique Value Proposition:

- Develop a unique value proposition for your side hustle. Clearly articulate what sets you apart from competitors. This could be in terms of product features, customer experience, pricing, or any other factor that creates a distinct identity for your venture.

6. SWOT Analysis:

- Conduct a SWOT analysis (Strengths, Weaknesses, Opportunities, Threats) for your side hustle and your competitors. This structured approach helps identify internal and external factors that can impact your business strategy.

7. Target Audience Insights:

- Gain insights into the target audience of your competitors. Understand their demographics, preferences, and behaviors. This knowledge enables you to tailor your marketing strategies and product offerings more effectively.

8. Gap Identification:

- Identify gaps in the market by assessing unmet needs or underserved segments. Gaps can arise from customer dissatisfaction, changing trends, or areas where competitors may have overlooked opportunities.

9. Innovating Solutions:

- Innovate solutions to address identified gaps. Your side hustle can thrive by offering something novel or by providing a better solution to existing problems. Consider how your venture can fill the voids you've identified.

10. Continuous Monitoring:
    - Establish a system for continuous monitoring of the competitive landscape. Markets evolve, and new players may enter. Regularly reassessing the competition and market gaps ensures your side hustle remains agile and responsive.

By systematically analyzing competition and gaps in the market, your side hustle gains a strategic advantage. This knowledge not only informs your business decisions but positions your venture as a solution-provider, capable of meeting the evolving needs of your target audience.

Chapter 4.

Planning and Setting Realistic Goals

- Crafting a Business Plan for Your Side Hustle

A well-crafted business plan is the roadmap that guides your side hustle toward success. Whether you're a seasoned entrepreneur or just starting, outlining your goals, strategies, and operational details in a business plan provides clarity and direction. Here's a step-by-step guide to help you craft a comprehensive business plan for your side hustle:

1. Executive Summary:

- Begin with an executive summary that succinctly captures the essence of your side hustle. Include your business idea, mission statement, target audience, and key objectives. This section serves as a snapshot of your entire business plan.

2. Business Description:
   - Provide a detailed description of your side hustle. Explain the nature of your products or services, the problem you aim to solve, and the unique value proposition that sets your venture apart in the market.

3. Market Analysis:
   - Conduct a thorough market analysis. Define your target market, analyze customer demographics, and assess competitors. Identify market trends, challenges, and opportunities that could impact your side hustle.

4. Organizational Structure:

- Outline the organizational structure of your side hustle. Define roles and responsibilities, and introduce key team members if applicable. Clarify how your business operates on a day-to-day basis.

5. Products or Services:
   - Provide detailed information about your products or services. Describe their features, benefits, and how they meet the needs of your target audience. Highlight any unique selling points that give you a competitive advantage.

6. Marketing and Sales Strategy:
   - Outline your marketing and sales strategies. Define how you will promote your side hustle, reach your target audience, and convert leads into customers. Include pricing strategies, distribution channels, and sales projections.

7. Funding Requirements:

- If applicable, detail your funding requirements. Specify the initial investment needed, potential sources of funding, and how the funds will be utilized. This section is crucial for attracting investors or securing loans.

8. Financial Projections:
- Present financial projections for your side hustle. Include income statements, balance sheets, and cash flow forecasts. This section demonstrates the financial viability and potential profitability of your venture.

9. Operational Plan:
- Provide an operational plan outlining the day-to-day activities required to run your side hustle. Address logistical considerations, production processes, and any partnerships or collaborations that support your operations.

10. Risk Management:

- Identify potential risks and how you plan to mitigate them. Address both internal and external risks that could impact your side hustle. A thoughtful risk management strategy enhances your preparedness for challenges.

11. Milestones and Goals:
    - Set specific milestones and goals for your side hustle. These could include product launch dates, revenue targets, customer acquisition goals, or any other key achievements. Clearly defined milestones help track progress.

12. Exit Strategy:
    - Although a side hustle is often a passion project, consider including an exit strategy. Define potential scenarios for exiting the business, whether through a sale, merger, or other means.

Crafting a business plan for your side hustle is not just a formality; it's a dynamic document that evolves with your venture. Regularly revisit and update your plan as your side hustle grows and market conditions change. A well-prepared business plan not only guides your current actions but also provides a valuable reference point for future decisions and strategic adjustments.

- Setting Achievable Milestones

Setting achievable milestones is a pivotal aspect of steering your side hustle toward success. These milestones serve as measurable checkpoints, providing clarity on your progress and guiding your efforts. Here's a guide to help you set realistic and impactful milestones for your side hustle:

1. Define Clear Objectives:

- Begin by defining clear and specific objectives for your side hustle. What do you aim to achieve in the short term and the long term? Objectives provide the foundation for setting meaningful milestones.

2. Break Down Larger Goals:

- Break down larger goals into smaller, manageable milestones. This step-by-step approach makes progress more tangible and allows you to celebrate achievements along the way.

3. Prioritize Milestones:

- Prioritize your milestones based on their significance and impact on your overall objectives. Identify key milestones that, when achieved, will significantly propel your side hustle forward.

4. Make Them Measurable:

- Ensure your milestones are measurable. Whether it's revenue targets, customer acquisition numbers, or product development milestones, having quantifiable metrics provides clarity on success.

5. Assign Timeframes:
- Assign realistic timeframes to each milestone. Consider the resources at your disposal, the complexity of tasks, and external factors that may influence your timeline. This helps in creating a feasible roadmap.

6. Consider Dependencies:
- Identify any dependencies between milestones. Some tasks may need to be completed before others can begin. Recognizing these dependencies helps in planning and ensures a smooth progression.

7. Align with Business Phases:

- Align milestones with different phases of your business. For instance, initial milestones might focus on product development and market entry, while later milestones could center around scaling, marketing, or diversification.

8. Celebrate Small Wins:
- Celebrate small wins along the way. Acknowledging and appreciating even minor achievements keeps motivation high and fosters a positive and productive work environment.

9. Adjust Based on Feedback:
- Be open to adjusting milestones based on feedback and changing circumstances. Flexibility is key in entrepreneurship, and the ability to adapt your plan enhances your side hustle's resilience.

10. Incorporate Learning Goals:
- Include learning goals as milestones. Whether it's acquiring a new skill,

understanding your target audience better, or implementing feedback, continuous learning is a valuable aspect of entrepreneurial growth.

11. Track and Evaluate:
- Implement a system to track and evaluate your progress regularly. Use tools, metrics, or project management software to assess how well you're meeting each milestone and make informed decisions accordingly.

12. Reflect and Iterate:
- Regularly reflect on your achievements and challenges. Consider what worked well, what could be improved, and how you can optimize your approach for future milestones. This reflective process contributes to ongoing refinement and growth.

Setting achievable milestones is not just about reaching the destination; it's about creating a roadmap that enhances your side hustle's journey. By carefully planning, measuring progress, and staying adaptable, you position your venture for sustained success and continuous improvement.

- Balancing Ambition with Realism

Achieving success in your side hustle requires a delicate balance between ambition and realism. While ambitious goals propel you forward, grounding them in reality ensures practicality and sustainability. Here's a guide to help you strike the right balance:

1. Define Clear Objectives:
   - Begin by defining clear and specific objectives for your side hustle. Ambitious objectives are inspiring, but they should also

be realistic and attainable within a given timeframe.

2. Assess Available Resources:

- Realistically assess the resources at your disposal. Consider your time, finances, skills, and network. Ambition should align with available resources to ensure feasibility.

3. Set Stretch Goals:

- Embrace ambition by setting stretch goals that challenge your capabilities. However, be mindful that these goals remain within the realm of possibility, encouraging growth without setting unrealistic expectations.

4. Break Down Larger Goals:

- Break down larger, ambitious goals into smaller, actionable steps. This not only makes the journey more manageable but also provides a clear roadmap for achieving your overarching ambitions.

5. Evaluate Time Commitments:

- Be realistic about the time commitments required. Balancing a side hustle with other responsibilities demands a practical assessment of the time you can realistically dedicate to your venture.

6. Prioritize:

- Prioritize your goals based on their impact on your overall vision. While some objectives may be more ambitious, others might be foundational. This prioritization helps in managing expectations and resources effectively.

7. Stay Adaptable:

- Ambition should not hinder adaptability. Be open to adjusting your goals based on feedback, changing market conditions, or unexpected challenges. Realism involves a willingness to pivot when necessary.

8. Assess Market Realities:

- Consider market realities when setting ambitious goals. Understanding your industry, competition, and market trends helps you set targets that are both ambitious and aligned with the dynamics of your business environment.

9. Seek Feedback:
- Seek feedback from mentors, peers, or industry experts. External perspectives can provide valuable insights into the realism of your ambitions. Constructive feedback guides you in refining your goals.

10. Monitor Progress:
- Regularly monitor your progress toward ambitious goals. Assess what's working well and where adjustments are needed. Realism involves an ongoing evaluation of your journey and a willingness to course-correct as needed.

11. Mitigate Risks:

- Realistically assess potential risks associated with your ambitious goals. Develop contingency plans and mitigation strategies. This proactive approach minimizes the impact of unforeseen challenges on your side hustle.

12. Celebrate Incremental Wins:
- Acknowledge and celebrate incremental wins along the way. Balancing ambition with realism involves appreciating the smaller achievements that collectively contribute to the larger vision.

By harmonizing ambition with realism, you create a sustainable and growth-oriented framework for your side hustle. The balance allows you to dream big, aspire for significant achievements, and yet remain rooted in practical steps that steadily propel your venture forward.

Chapter 5.

Building Your Brand and Online Presence

- Creating a Unique Brand Identity

In the digital age, building a strong brand and online presence is instrumental for the success of your side hustle. Establishing a unique brand identity not only distinguishes your venture in a crowded marketplace but also fosters connections with your target audience. Here's a guide to creating a distinctive brand identity for your side hustle:

1. Define Your Brand Values:
   - Start by defining your brand values. What principles and beliefs underpin your

side hustle? Aligning your brand with core values provides a foundation for authenticity and connection with your audience.

2. Understand Your Target Audience:
   - Gain a deep understanding of your target audience. Know their demographics, preferences, and pain points. Tailoring your brand identity to resonate with your audience's needs fosters a more meaningful connection.

3. Craft a Unique Value Proposition:
   - Clearly articulate your unique value proposition. What sets your side hustle apart from competitors? Whether it's innovative features, exceptional quality, or a distinctive brand story, communicate what makes your brand unique.

4. Develop a Memorable Logo and Visual Elements:
   - Invest in a memorable logo and visual elements that reflect your brand identity.

Consistent use of colors, fonts, and imagery creates a cohesive and recognizable brand image across various platforms.

5. Create Compelling Brand Messaging:
   - Craft compelling brand messaging that communicates your story and resonates with your audience. Convey the benefits of your products or services and how they align with the values of your target customers.

6. Establish Consistent Brand Voice:
   - Define and establish a consistent brand voice. Whether your brand is casual, formal, humorous, or educational, maintaining a consistent tone across all communication channels enhances brand recognition and trust.

7. Build a Responsive Website:
   - Invest in a responsive website that reflects your brand identity. Ensure that the design, layout, and content align with your

values and effectively convey your offerings. A user-friendly website enhances the online experience for your audience.

8. Leverage Social Media Platforms:
- Utilize social media platforms strategically. Choose platforms that align with your target audience and industry. Consistent and engaging content on social media enhances your brand visibility and fosters community engagement.

9. Implement Content Marketing:
- Implement a content marketing strategy. Create valuable and relevant content that showcases your expertise and aligns with your brand values. Blog posts, videos, and other content contribute to building authority and trust.

10. Encourage User-generated Content:
- Encourage user-generated content. Actively engage with your audience, and showcase their positive experiences with

your brand. User-generated content not only serves as testimonials but also builds a sense of community.

11. Collaborate and Partner:
- Collaborate with influencers or other businesses that align with your brand values. Partnerships can expand your reach and introduce your brand to new audiences while reinforcing your identity through association.

12. Gather and Respond to Feedback:
- Actively seek and respond to customer feedback. Understanding how your audience perceives your brand allows you to make informed adjustments and continually refine your brand identity.

Building a unique brand identity is an ongoing process that evolves with your side hustle. By consistently embodying your brand values, engaging with your audience, and adapting to market dynamics, you a brand that not only stands out but also resonates with and captivates your target customers.

- Establishing an Online Presence

In the digital era, establishing a robust online presence is vital for the success of your side hustle. An effective online presence not only enhances visibility but also enables you to connect with a global audience and build credibility. Here's a comprehensive guide to help you establish and optimize your online presence:

1. Create a Professional Website:
   - Start by creating a professional and user-friendly website. Your website serves as the online hub for your side hustle,

providing information about your products or services, contact details, and a platform for potential customers to engage with your brand.

2. Optimize for Search Engines (SEO):
   - Implement search engine optimization (SEO) strategies to improve your website's visibility on search engines. Use relevant keywords, create high-quality content, and ensure your website is structured for optimal search engine rankings.

3. Leverage Social Media Platforms:
   - Identify and leverage social media platforms relevant to your target audience. Establish a presence on platforms such as Facebook, Instagram, Twitter, or LinkedIn. Tailor your content to each platform and engage with your audience regularly.

4. Develop a Content Strategy:
   - Develop a content strategy that aligns with your brand and resonates with your

audience. Regularly publish blog posts, articles, videos, or other forms of content that showcase your expertise, provide value, and drive engagement.

5. Utilize Email Marketing:
   - Implement email marketing campaigns to nurture relationships with your audience. Build a subscriber list and send newsletters, product updates, or exclusive offers. Email marketing is a powerful tool for fostering customer loyalty.

6. Invest in Online Advertising:
   - Consider online advertising to increase visibility and reach a broader audience. Platforms like Google Ads or social media advertising allow you to target specific demographics and measure the effectiveness of your campaigns.

7. Engage in Online Communities:
   - Join and engage in online communities relevant to your industry or niche.

Participate in discussions, share insights, and build relationships. Being an active member of communities establishes your authority and expands your network.

8. Implement E-commerce Solutions:
  - If applicable, implement e-commerce solutions on your website. Streamline the online purchasing process, provide secure payment options, and ensure a seamless user experience for customers interested in buying your products.

9. Showcase Customer Testimonials:
  - Display customer testimonials on your website. Positive reviews build trust and credibility. Consider creating a dedicated section for testimonials or featuring them strategically on product pages.

10. Monitor Online Reputation:
  - Monitor your online reputation by regularly checking reviews and mentions of your brand. Respond to customer feedback,

whether positive or negative, to demonstrate your commitment to customer satisfaction.

11. Offer Valuable Resources:
- Provide valuable resources on your website. This could include downloadable guides, whitepapers, or any content that adds value to your audience. Offering resources positions your brand as an authority in your field.

12. Stay Consistent Across Platforms:
- Maintain consistency across all online platforms. From your website to social media profiles, ensure a cohesive brand image. Consistency fosters recognition and reinforces your brand identity.

Establishing a strong online presence is an ongoing effort that requires adaptability and a commitment to staying current with digital trends. By strategically utilizing various online channels and consistently delivering value to your audience, you position your side hustle for sustained growth and success in the digital landscape.

- Leveraging Social Media for Marketing

Social media has become a powerhouse for marketing, providing businesses, including side hustles, with unparalleled opportunities to connect with their audience, build brand awareness, and drive engagement. Here's a comprehensive guide on how to effectively leverage social media for marketing your side hustle:

1. Identify Your Target Audience:
- Begin by identifying your target audience. Understand their demographics, interests, and online behaviors. This

knowledge will guide your social media strategy, ensuring that your content resonates with the right audience.

2. Choose the Right Platforms:

- Select social media platforms that align with your target audience and business goals. Whether it's Facebook, Instagram, Twitter, LinkedIn, or others, focus on platforms where your audience is most active.

3. Create a Content Calendar:

- Develop a content calendar to plan and organize your social media posts. Consistent posting is key to maintaining an active and engaging online presence. Use the calendar to strategize content themes, promotions, and timely posts.

4. Craft Engaging Content:

- Create engaging and visually appealing content. This could include images, videos, infographics, or written posts. Tailor your content to each platform, keeping in mind the preferences and behaviors of your audience on each channel.

5. Utilize Hashtags Strategically:
- Use hashtags strategically to increase the discoverability of your content. Research relevant and trending hashtags in your industry and incorporate them into your posts to broaden your reach.

6. Foster Community Engagement:
- Encourage community engagement by responding to comments, messages, and mentions. Foster a sense of community around your brand by actively participating in conversations and acknowledging your audience.

7. Run Contests and Giveaways:
- Running contests and giveaways is an effective way to boost engagement and expand your reach. Encourage participants

to share your content or tag friends for a chance to win, creating a viral effect.

8. Collaborate with Influencers:
   - Consider collaborating with influencers in your niche. Influencers can introduce your brand to their followers, providing a trusted endorsement that can significantly impact brand awareness and credibility.

9. Utilize Paid Advertising:
   - Explore paid advertising options on social media platforms. Paid ads allow you to target specific demographics, interests, and behaviors, ensuring that your content reaches the most relevant audience.

10. Monitor Analytics and Metrics:
   - Regularly monitor analytics and metrics to assess the performance of your social media efforts. Track engagement, reach, and conversions to understand what works best and make data-driven adjustments.

11. Showcase Behind-the-Scenes:

- Humanize your brand by showcasing behind-the-scenes content. Introduce your team, share your creative process, or provide glimpses of day-to-day operations. Authenticity builds a stronger connection with your audience.

12. Stay Informed on Trends:

- Stay informed about social media trends and algorithm changes. The landscape is dynamic, and staying current ensures that your strategy remains effective and adapts to evolving user behaviors.

Leveraging social media for marketing is a dynamic and ever-evolving process. By understanding your audience, creating compelling content, and actively engaging with your community, you can harness the power of social media to elevate your side hustle's visibility and impact.

Chapter 6.

Financial Management and Scaling

- Budgeting for Your Side Hustle

Effective budgeting is a cornerstone of success for any side hustle. It provides a clear financial roadmap, helps in making informed decisions, and ensures that your venture remains financially sustainable. Here's a guide to help you navigate the budgeting process for your side hustle:

1. Define Your Goals and Expenses:

- Begin by clearly defining your side hustle goals and identifying your expenses. Categorize your expenses into fixed costs (e.g., website hosting, subscriptions) and variable costs (e.g., marketing, materials).

2. Estimate Income and Revenue Streams:

- Project your potential income and revenue streams. Consider factors like product/service pricing, sales projections, and any additional income streams (e.g., affiliate marketing, collaborations) that contribute to your side hustle's revenue.

3. Create a Realistic Revenue Forecast:

- Develop a realistic revenue forecast based on your market research and business model. Be conservative in your estimates to account for uncertainties and unexpected challenges.

4. Prioritize Essential Expenses:

- Prioritize essential expenses that are critical for your side hustle's operations.

These may include product development, marketing, website maintenance, and any other costs directly linked to generating revenue.

5. Allocate Funds for Marketing:

- Allocate a portion of your budget for marketing efforts. Effective marketing is essential for building brand awareness, reaching your target audience, and driving sales. Consider both online and offline marketing channels.

6. Build an Emergency Fund:

- Set aside funds for an emergency fund. Unforeseen expenses or changes in the market can impact your side hustle, and having a financial buffer provides stability during challenging times.

7. Consider Taxes and Legal Compliance:

- Factor in taxes and legal compliance costs. Understand the tax obligations related to your side hustle and allocate funds accordingly. Consult with a tax professional if needed to ensure compliance.

8. Monitor Cash Flow Regularly:

- Regularly monitor your cash flow. This involves tracking both incoming and outgoing funds to ensure that your side hustle maintains healthy liquidity. Address any discrepancies promptly.

9. Evaluate Return on Investment (ROI):

- Evaluate the return on investment for your expenditures. Assess the effectiveness of marketing campaigns, product launches, or any initiatives contributing to your side hustle's growth. Adjust your budget based on the ROI analysis.

10. Adjust and Iterate:

- Be flexible and willing to adjust your budget as needed. Market conditions, customer preferences, and external factors can change, requiring you to adapt your financial plan to ensure long-term sustainability.

11. Separate Personal and Business Finances:

- Keep personal and business finances separate. This not only simplifies accounting but also provides a clear distinction between your side hustle's income and your expenses.

12. Invest in Professional Development:

- Allocate funds for your professional development. This may include courses, workshops, or resources that enhance your skills and knowledge, contributing to the overall growth of your side hustle.

Creating and sticking to a budget is an ongoing process that requires diligence and adaptability. By establishing a solid financial foundation, you position your side hustle for stability, growth, and resilience in the dynamic landscape of entrepreneurship.

- Pricing Strategies and Revenue Streams

Pricing your products or services strategically is a critical component of running a successful side hustle. It not only determines your revenue but also influences customer perception and competitive positioning. Here's a guide to help you navigate pricing strategies and establish diverse revenue streams for your side hustle:

1. Understand Cost Structures:
   - Begin by thoroughly understanding your cost structures. Identify all the costs associated with producing and delivering your products or services, including production costs, materials, labor, and overhead.

2. Calculate Break-Even Point:

- Calculate your break-even point to determine the minimum revenue required to cover costs. This analysis helps set a baseline for pricing and ensures that your side hustle operates profitably.

3. Research Market Prices:

- Research market prices for similar products or services. Understanding what competitors charge provides insights into industry standards and helps you position your offerings competitively.

4. Value-Based Pricing:

- Consider value-based pricing, where the price is determined by the perceived value your product or service provides to customers. Focus on the benefits and unique value proposition to justify a premium price.

5. Cost-Plus Pricing:

- Implement cost-plus pricing by adding a markup percentage to your production costs. This straightforward approach ensures that your pricing covers both variable and fixed costs while providing a profit margin.

6. Dynamic Pricing:

- Explore dynamic pricing strategies, where prices adjust based on factors like demand, seasonality, or customer segments. Dynamic pricing allows for flexibility and optimization in response to market changes.

7. Bundle and Upsell:

- Create bundled offerings and upsell opportunities. Bundling products or services at a slightly discounted price encourages customers to purchase more, while upselling introduces higher-value options for increased revenue.

8. Subscription Models:

- Introduce subscription models for recurring revenue. Subscriptions provide a steady income stream and enhance customer loyalty. Consider offering tiered subscription plans with varying features.

9. Freemium or Tiered Pricing:
   - Implement a freemium or tiered pricing model, where you offer basic services for free and charge for premium features. This strategy attracts a wider audience while capturing revenue from those willing to pay for additional benefits.

10. Discounts and Promotions:
    - Strategically use discounts and promotions to stimulate sales. Consider limited-time offers, introductory pricing, or loyalty programs to incentivize purchases and create a sense of urgency.

11. Evaluate Customer Feedback:
    - Pay attention to customer feedback regarding pricing. Understand their

perception of value and willingness to pay. Use this feedback to iterate on your pricing strategy and make informed adjustments.

12. Diversify Revenue Streams:

- Diversify your revenue streams to reduce dependency on a single source. This could include exploring new product lines, entering different markets, or offering complementary services that align with your core business.

13. Continuous Monitoring and Adjustments:

- Continuously monitor the performance of your pricing strategy. Stay informed about market trends, customer preferences, and competitor actions. Be prepared to make adjustments to your pricing strategy as needed.

Establishing effective pricing strategies and diverse revenue streams requires a balance between covering costs, providing value, and staying competitive. By adopting a thoughtful approach, regularly assessing market dynamics, and being responsive to customer needs, you position your side hustle for sustainable growth and profitability.

- Scaling Your Side Hustle for Long-Term Success

Scaling your side hustle is a pivotal step toward long-term success. It involves expanding your operations, increasing revenue, and solidifying your presence in the market. Here's a comprehensive guide to help you navigate the process of scaling your side hustle:

1. Evaluate Scalability Potential:

- Begin by evaluating the scalability potential of your side hustle. Consider factors such as demand, market size, and the feasibility of expanding your current offerings.

2. Optimize Operations:
- Streamline and optimize your operations to handle increased demand. This may involve improving efficiency, automating certain processes, and investing in tools or technologies that enhance productivity.

3. Diversify Product or Service Offerings:
- Explore opportunities to diversify your product or service offerings. Introducing complementary products or expanding your range can attract new customers and increase overall revenue.

4. Expand Your Market Reach:
- Expand your market reach by targeting new customer segments or entering different geographic markets. Conduct

market research to identify untapped opportunities and tailor your strategies accordingly.

5. Invest in Marketing and Promotion:

- Increase your investment in marketing and promotion. Scaling often requires a broader reach, and strategic marketing efforts can elevate brand awareness, attract a larger audience, and drive sales.

6. Build Strategic Partnerships:

- Explore strategic partnerships that can facilitate growth. Collaborate with other businesses, influencers, or organizations that align with your brand. Partnerships can provide access to new audiences and resources.

7. Enhance Online Presence:

- Strengthen your online presence to reach a wider audience. Invest in digital marketing, social media strategies, and search engine optimization to maximize your visibility and attract online customers.

8. Optimize Customer Experience:

- Prioritize customer experience optimization. Satisfied customers are more likely to become repeat buyers and brand advocates, contributing to sustained growth. Seek feedback and continually refine your processes based on customer insights.

9. Implement Technology Solutions:

- Integrate technology solutions to support scalability. Whether it's upgrading your e-commerce platform, implementing a customer relationship management (CRM) system, or leveraging automation tools, technology can enhance efficiency.

10. Build a Strong Team:

- As your side hustle grows, build a strong and dedicated team. Assess the skills needed for expansion and hire individuals who complement your strengths. A capable team is instrumental in scaling operations successfully.

11. Monitor Key Performance Indicators (KPIs):

- Establish and monitor key performance indicators (KPIs) relevant to your scaling goals. Regularly assess metrics such as customer acquisition cost, conversion rates, and revenue per customer to gauge performance and identify areas for improvement.

12. Manage Finances Prudently:

- Manage your finances prudently during the scaling process. Keep a close eye on cash flow, allocate resources wisely, and be mindful of potential financial challenges that may arise during the expansion.

13. Plan for Scalability Challenges:

- Anticipate and plan for scalability challenges. Whether it's increased customer support demands, logistics complexities, or supply chain issues, having contingency plans in place helps you navigate challenges effectively.

14. Stay Agile and Adaptive:
   - Maintain agility and adaptability. The business landscape evolves, and being responsive to changes ensures that your side hustle can adjust to shifting market dynamics and consumer trends.

Scaling your side hustle is a continuous journey that requires strategic planning, a customer-centric approach, and a willingness to embrace change. By systematically implementing scalable practices and staying attuned to your market, you position your side hustle for sustained growth and long-term success.